EXPLORING REALISTIC FICTION

SCHOLASTIC INC.

EXPLORING REALISTIC FICTION

PERMISSIONS–"Chinese New Year" from *In the Year of the Boar and Jackie Robinson* by Bette Bao Lord. Copyright © 1984. Reprinted by permission of Harper Collins Junior Books. "We Haven't Much Time" from *My Name is San Ho* by Jayne Pettit. Copyright © 1992. Reprinted by permission of Scholastic, Inc. From *Blue Skye* by Lael Littke. Copyright © 1990. Reprinted by permission of Scholastic, Inc.

ART AND PHOTO CREDITS—Cover: illustration by Donna Perrone; Title Page: illustration by Chi Chung; pages 4, 12 and 18: illustrations by Yan Nascimbene; pages 20 and 26: illustrations by Chi Chung; pages 32, 40 and 46: illustrations by Donna Perrone.

ISBN 0-590-49296-9

CONTENTS

IN THE
YEAR OF THE BOAR
AND
JACKIE ROBINSON
by
Bette Bao Lord

CHINESE NEW YEAR

In the Year of the Dog, 4645, there lived halfway across the world from New York a girl called Sixth Cousin. Otherwise known as Bandit.

One winter morning, a letter arrived at the House of Wong from her father, who had been traveling the four seas. On the stamp sat an ugly, bald bird. The paper was blue. When Mother read it, she smiled. But the words made Grandmother cry and Grandfather angry. No one gave Sixth Cousin even the smallest hint of why.

It is so unfair, she thought. Must I drool like Chow Chow, eyeing each mouthful until someone is good and ready to toss a scrap my way? If Father was here, he'd tell. He would never treat me like a child, like a girl, like a nobody.

Still, Bandit dared not ask. How many times had she been told that no proper member of an upright

Confucian family ever questioned the conduct of elders? Or that children must wait until invited to speak? Countless times. Only the aged were considered wise. Even the opinion of her father, the youngest son of the Patriarch, did not matter. No wonder he had gone away to seek his fortune.

She tried to pretend nothing had happened, but it was hard. All day, the elders behaved unnaturally in her presence. No unintended slights, quick nods, easy smiles, teasing remarks or harsh words. They were so kind, too kind. Bandit felt as if she had sprouted a second head, and they were all determined to ignore politely the unsightly growth.

That evening, as she and Fourth Cousin sat on the bed playing pick-up-beans, she confided in her best friend. "Something's happened. Something big has happened!"

"Oh?" said the older girl. "You are always imagining things! Remember the time you told everyone there was a goldfish swimming in the bamboo trees? It was only a fallen kite. Remember the time you overheard the cook plotting to murder the washerwoman? He was only sharpening his cleaver to kill a hen."

Bandit scowled as she scattered the dried lima beans. "That was then. Now is now!"

"All right, all right," sighed her dearest friend. "What has happened now?"

"That's it. I don't know," she answered.

"Well then, let's play. My turn. Sixies."

"No!" shouted Bandit, grabbing the other girl's

hands. "Think! Think! What would make Mother smile, Grandmother cry and Grandfather angry?"

Fourth Cousin shrugged her shoulders and began to unbraid her hair. She was always fussing with her hair.

Bandit thought and thought, annoyed at her friend's silence, sorry that no matter how Fourth Cousin tried she would never be pretty.

Soon the coals in the brazier were dying, and suddenly the room was cold. The cousins scrambled under the covers. The beans tumbled onto the floor. Bandit knew she should pick them up, but she just stayed put. She had thinking to do.

Finally Bandit had the answer. Fourth Cousin was asleep.

"Wake up! Wake up!"

"Mmmmmmmmmmm?"

"Listen. I've got it. Remember the time the enemy planes bombed the city for two straight days and we had to hide in the caves with only hard-boiled eggs to eat? What happened when we came home?"

"Who cares?"

"Father bought us that pony of a dog. Mother thought it was cute and smiled. But Grandmother was frightened and cried and hid behind the moon gate. And Grandfather was very angry. He said, 'Youngest Son, are you mad? Unless you mean for us to eat that beast, take him away. Take him away this minute.' His voice was as cold as the northwest wind." Bandit stood up and threaded her hands into her sleeves as Grandfather did. She cleared her throat the way he did whenever he was displeased, and stomped up and down the bed.

Fourth Cousin never opened an eye. She turned on her side and curled up like a shrimp.

Bandit pounced on her. "Don't you see? Father is bringing the dog back."

"Never!"

Bandit thought it over and sighed. "You're right. You're always right." Quietly, very quietly, she slipped under the covers.

Sleep still would not come. Bandit heard the sounds of laughter and voices, footfalls and bicycle bells, as guests departed from one court, then another. It was the season for merrymaking, when the New Year approaches and old debts are paid. At last the lanterns along the garden walk were snuffed out, and the room was dark. Bandit reached out. Fourth Cousin's hand was warm.

Through the wall came the faint strains of a song. Mother was playing Father's record again.

The music carried Bandit away, thousands of miles to the sea. Its waters were not muddy like the River of Golden Sands that churned at the bottom of the Mountain of Ten Thousand Steps on which the House of Wong was perched. The sea was calm; deep green like jade. As far as the heavens, the skies soared. In the distance, something blue. A boat in the shape of a bird. Slowly it floated toward shore. She shaded her eyes to get a better look. On the deck was Father. She shouted and waved, but he did not seem to hear.

"Father! Father!" She shouted until she was hoarse. Then she ran into the sea, forgetting she could not swim. Soon he was just a fingertip away. "Father! Father!"

Her cries angered the sleeping demons of the deep and they sent a wall of water to quiet the intruder . .

Splash! She awoke. Her face was wet.

"Look what you've made me do, you Bandit!"

She sat up to find Fourth Cousin gone and Awaiting Marriage, the servant, sprawled on the floor. Beside the old woman was a shattered water urn. All about, the offending beans.

Before Bandit could apologize, Awaiting Marriage screwed up her skinny face and wailed. The sight was ugly enough to frighten the devil himself. Cook was right. One hundred wedding trunks could not buy Awaiting Marriage even a hunchbacked, lame-footed husband.

"Bandit, I've got you this time. This time you have to answer to your grandmother. I'm going to show her the pieces!" The servant stood up, shaking a fragment in Bandit's face.

Bandit brushed her hand away. "It's nothing but crockery. No Ming urn!"

Awaiting Marriage squeezed out a wicked smile. "Aha! You've forgotten it's New Year's time. Yes, Bandit, New Year's time." Giggling, the servant scurried out.

Amitabha! Bandit was in trouble, deep trouble.

Grandmother was the Matriarch of the House of Wong. What she ordered was always done. What she said was always so. How many times had she warned against breaking things during the holidays? It would bring bad luck, bad luck for the next three hundred and sixty-five days. And if anything made Grandmother unreasonable, it was bad luck.

Quickly, Bandit got out of bed, used what was left in Fourth Cousin's water urn to wash, dressed, plaited her hair and then began seriously to clean the room. That was another of Grandmother's dictums. Not a speck of dust. Not a misplaced article. Everything must be in harmony to welcome the New Year.

As she was straightening out the shoes in the bottom of the tall rosewood bureau, Awaiting Marriage appeared at the door. She grinned as if greeting the matchmaker. "Young Mistress," she said, gloating. "Young Mistress, the Matriarch wishes to see you in her quarters."

"Now?"

"Now." With an extravagant bow, the tattletale removed herself.

Bandit felt as if she had been summoned by an irate emperor. This time the punishment would be more than harsh words or three strokes of a bamboo cane. Much more. But she had to obey. No one ever disobeyed the Matriarch. Quickly she ran to the washstand and tucked a towel inside the seat of her pants. Still . . .there must be some way to soften Grandmother's heart. She must think. And quickly, before another offense was added to the first. Think. Who could help?

Yes, of course, naturally. Ninth Cousin, otherwise known as Precious Coins. He was the baby of the clan. The favored grandchild. Whenever Bandit needed a few pennies to buy melon seeds or candied plums, she sent Precious Coins to ask Grandmother for them. The Matriarch never refused him. If he would shed a bucket of tears for Bandit, perhaps her life would be spared.

Where could that fat boy be? He hated to walk, loved being carried. With all the cousins getting ready for the festivities, he was probably still sitting on his bed like a buddha, waiting for a pair of feet.

She ran out the door, along the gallery past Mother's room, through the rock garden into the next court, which belonged to Third Uncle. She tip-toed past his study. Uncle hated to be disturbed when he was doing accounts. And that's all he ever did. She heard him muttering as he clicked the beads on his abacus, figuring out new ways to pocket a cent. Poor Third Aunt. No matter how she screamed and schemed, her husband refused to loosen his purse strings. Unlike Father, he never squandered money for gifts. But he seldom reaped joy either.

Precious Coins was sitting on his bed. As soon as Bandit stepped into his room, he held out his arms. She could not resist giving him a big hug. He was cute as a dumpling and just as round.

"See Grandmother now?"

"Yes. But no pennies today. When I set you down, you must hold on to my leg. Don't let go, no matter what. A new game, see?"

"Hold leg. No let go."

"If you let go, you lose."

"No let go." Precious Coins held up his arms again.

Scooping him up, she walked slowly along the pathway past the lotus pond and crossed the half-moon bridge to the Matriarch's quarters.

At the threshold, Bandit hesitated. What took more courage—to enter or to run away? Inside sat all the women of the older generation, even Grand-grand-grand Auntie, who was ninety-three. It only proved Grandmother's warning to be true. Bad luck.

IN THE YEAR OF THE BOAR

It was already here.

"Granddaughter, you may come in."

Holding Precious Coins even tighter, Bandit inched toward the carved ebony chair in the center of the room. She kept her eyes on Grandmother's bound feet, which rested on a stool.

She set the boy down. At once he plopped to the floor and put his arms around her left leg.

"Good morning, Grandmother," she whispered, still keeping her eyes on Grandmother's feet. They were very tiny, like little red peppers.

"Look at me, child. I have something important to say."

One hundred lashes? Ten thousand characters to copy? One hundred thousand hours in her room? If only she had picked up the beans.

Blinking away the tears, Bandit looked up. Her eyes met the Matriarch's. No one spoke. Bandit looked around, searching for a friendly face among the women. No one smiled. Not even Mother.

"Granddaughter, today is one of the saddest days in my long life, in all our lives. You, my sixth grandchild, must go away, far away. . . ."

No! How can I? Bandit thought. I am too young. Who will take care of me? A tear fell, then another.

"Grandmother," she begged. "Let me have another chance. I will never, ever, as long as I live, break another thing during the holidays. I promise. Please don't send me away."

"What are you talking about? I am not sending you away. You are going away because your father has sent for you and your mother. He has decided not to return to Chungking. He plans to make America his home. Your grandfather has agreed."

The letter! No wonder Mother had smiled, Grandmother had cried and Grandfather had been so angry. Oh, Father, she thought. At long last, we'll be together again!

Bandit could not help smiling. She was brimful of happiness. But then she saw the sadness on Grandmother's face and ran to comfort her.

Boom! Bandit fell. True to his word, Precious Coins had not let go of her leg.

Then all the women of the House of Wong gathered around to fuss over her.

"Oh, you poor thing!" they cried. "What's to become of you?"

"Exiled like a criminal to a distant land."

"With no clan to nurture you. Surrounded by strangers."

"Strangers who aren't even Chinese."

"And those cowboys and Indians. What kind of place is that for a child to grow up in? Dodging bullets and arrows?"

"You'll starve! Imagine eating nothing but warm puppies and raw meat!"

"How will you become civilized? America does not honor Confucius. America is foreign, so foreign."

On and on they went, wailing like paid mourners at a funeral. But Bandit was not afraid. She had faith in her father. Nothing awful will happen, she told herself. No bad luck. The Year of the Boar would bring travel, adventure and double happiness.

The final day of the Year of the Dog lasted until dawn. No one slept. Not even Precious Coins. For tradition had long decreed that a bad dream on any New Year's Eve was an omen of bad tomorrows. To make sure no one had a nightmare, all the beds in the House of Wong stood empty until the skies were lit by the dawn and the danger passed.

The lofty Hall of Ancestors was festooned with holiday banners and graced with clansmen from near and far. They formed clusters of color like the glass pieces in a kaleidoscope. Everyone's gown was of bright silk or brocade, and many were embroidered with gold and silver threads and lined in fur, or stitched with sequins and pearls.

A few gowns, like Bandit's, betrayed the twelve-course dinner the clansmen had consumed earlier. It did not matter. At the New Year's feast no one ever scolded, even if a barbarian should wash his face in the soup. A few faces, like Bandit's, could use a washing, even in soup. They were streaked with ash, for they had leaned too close to the sizzle of fire-crackers. But even so, no cross words. On New Year's Eve, exceptions were the rule.

Gamblers seated at a dozen tables chatted and cheered as they vied at mah-jongg, cards and rhyming couplets, while would-be singing warriors and courtesans tagged after the tunes the musicians played and the servants, spinning like tops, circled the floor with drinks and delicacies. At each stop they collected a generous tip. Near daybreak of New Year's Day, even Third Uncle forgot himself.

Before the altar, which was laden with offerings for the ancestors, Grandfather sat, telling stories to the very old and the very young.

Many in his audience were fighting sleep. Their stomachs were filled with sweets . . . their pockets with red envelopes containing money from the elders . . . their heads with stories of monkey kings and fox fairies, noble ministers and celestial fools, loyal sons, forgetful magpies, the weaving maid who lived on the far side of the River of Stars. No wonder they drooped.

Not Bandit. She was wide awake, sitting cross-legged holding hands with Grand-grand Uncle and his wife of sixty years who, for as long as Bandit could recall, had refused to address her husband. Both the old artist and the former beauty had long forgotten his misdeed. The date of it, however, was enshrined in memory, and dubbed "Foul Friday." Perhaps, in the beginning, the wife might have relented. Then it became unthinkable. Now, in his old age, Grand-grand Uncle delighted in painting Grand-grand Auntie's portrait. Sometimes with warts. Sometimes with big feet or donkey grins. Always fanciful. Bandit thought each picture worth ten thousand laughs. Secretly she collected them, whispering to Grand-grand Auntie that she did so on her behalf. Thus, both artist and subject adored her. Thus, Bandit had become their official go-between.

". . . And so finally the worthy peasant could sleep peacefully in his grave."

Everyone applauded. Glancing up at the feuding husband and wife, Bandit saw tears in their eyes. If only, she thought, if only they could be friends again before I go away. Then they will not need a go-between. For the first time, Bandit felt a little bit sad to be going away.

Grandfather tapped his pipe on the arm of his chair, calling for attention. Suddenly, the Hall was still.

"It is almost time to go to bed, my clansmen. But before we can, there is something we must do. Sixth Cousin, rise and come to my side."

Bandit jumped to her feet and obeyed. Grandfather was the Patriarch of the clan, even more powerful than Grandmother. Everyone was now looking her way. Bandit blushed.

"Now, now, my child," Grandfather said with a smile, "since when have you become so shy?"

Everyone laughed, the cousins the loudest.

Tapping his pipe again, Grandfather continued. "As you know, my youngest son's wife and daughter will be leaving us this week. There will still be time enough to say a proper good-bye. But we must not send Sixth Cousin away without giving her an official name. Bandit will not do, will it?"

"No!" shouted the House of Wong.

"So, tell me my child, do you have a preference?"

"I, Grandfather?"

"Who else?"

Bandit looked to the rafters, as if a hint might be hidden there. Everyone waited quietly. Finally she replied, "Grandfather, since I am going to America, I would like an American name."

Some nodded approval. Others shook their heads. An American name!

Grandfather stroked his white beard. Then he said, "American name it is."

Now everyone nodded approval.

Bandit clapped. Fourth Cousin did too. My dearest friend, Bandit thought. I wish you were going with us. Again, she felt sad.

"Any suggestions, my child?" Grandfather asked.

She had not been prepared for that! Everyone

knew she did not speak English, but if she admitted it now everyone would enjoy a big laugh just the same. She looked at the rafters again. I must know an American name, she thought. I must.

Suddenly one came to her.

"How about Uncle Sam?" she shouted.

All laughed until some cried.

Bandit felt that her face was as red as a fried lobster.

Grandfather came to her rescue. "I, myself, do not care for the sound of it. How about something more melodious?"

Think! She must know another American name. Then it came to her. Yes, that was it. Everyone loved her movies. She was just about the most famous movie star in all the world.

"Shirley Temple!"

For a minute no one moved. Then Grandfather applauded. Then so did everyone else.

Grandfather tapped his pipe once more, calling the clansmen to order. Straightening his back, he pronounced the official words. "I, as Patriarch, do hereby advise my clansmen that my sixth grandchild, the thirty-third member of the House of Wong now living under the ancestral roofs, and one of the thirty-ninth generation registered in the Clan Book, will now be known as Shirley Temple Wong."

MY NAME IS SAN HO

by

Jayne Pettit

"WE HAVEN'T MUCH TIME"

The war had gone badly during the three years I had been in Saigon. The North Vietnamese had pushed steadily southward, crushing the port city of Da Nang and the provincial capitals of Tam Ky and Quang Ngai. This I learned from Kim Be's refugees and from several of the new students in my class at the convent school. Our ancient city of Hue—the city of scholars—had fallen to the Communists, too.

As I lay on my mat, I heard the soft sounds of Kim Be's sandals as she entered the room and moved toward me. "Quickly, San Ho," she whispered as she touched my arm gently. "We haven't much time."

Silently, I rolled my mat into a tight bundle and reached for my cloth sack. In it were the few belongings I owned—my mother's letters, the altar candle Grandfather had given me, and the crumpled sheet of paper containing Ong Thay's poems.

I followed Kim Be into the next room and sat down at the table, on which she had placed a small bowl of rice mixed with a portion of nuoc mam, a fish sauce we used to flavor our food. I ate hurriedly, for I knew that we would leave as soon as the curfew lifted, and I had no idea how long it would be before I would eat again.

"Kim Be?" I finally whispered.

"Yes, San Ho."

"Please, tell me again the story of my mother. And tell me, please, how you know she *really* is waiting for me in America."

Kim Be settled into her steady pace and once again began the story she had first told me the week before.

"Two years ago, in 1973—the year after your mother brought you to Saigon to stay with me—terrible things were happening in your village. The rice fields were destroyed by air attacks, and the vegetable crops and fruit trees were black with the poison from the chemicals that had been sprayed by the helicopters. The villagers had little help from the government, and there was no medical aid to ease their pain."

"Tell me again about Grandfather, Kim Be. Tell me how he died."

"One day, several weeks after you had gone, your grandfather walked to the well in the center of the hamlet to draw water. Without warning, two jets appeared overhead. With nowhere to hide, your grandfather was trapped. After a few minutes, the planes disappeared, and two peasants ran to the well to find his body, the water bucket still clutched in his hand. All of this is sadly true, according to your mother's letter to us from America."

"Do you think the war will end, Kim Be?"

Kim turned her head toward me. "Do all twelve-year-olds ask as many questions as you? This is one that I cannot answer. No one can."

"Please go on, Kim Be," I said, urging her to finish her story.

"Soon after your grandfather's death, a detachment of American Marines came to the village. They told the peasants they would have to leave because it was no longer safe to live there. The Marines told your mother and the others that they would be taken to a strategic hamlet.

"Your mother and several of the women refused to go. They said they would not live behind barbed wire. What would they do in a place where there were no rice fields to tend and no crops to raise? And how could anyone save them from the bombs that fell from the sky?"

"That was when Mother decided to go to the American base, which was near Mi Hung, wasn't it?" I remembered.

"That's right, San Ho. There was a chance for her to find work at the base. She was also given two rooms to share with five other women who had gone with her."

"Was that where my mother met the American?" I asked.

"Yes," Kim replied. "And when he was given orders to return to America, they decided to marry and leave Vietnam together."

"But why—why didn't my mother come to get me before she left?" I asked, knowing the answer but eager to have it explained once again.

"Because your village was destroyed by the Viet Cong after the people had moved to the strategic hamlet, and there were no records of your birth in Mi Hung. There was no way that your mother could prove to the authorities in Saigon that you were her son. I'm afraid the officials who take care of matters like this make it quite complicated! And so, your mother's letters to the government went unanswered, and permission for you to leave with her did not come.

"Then one day, your mother received a letter from Saigon assuring her that you would be allowed to go within a matter of weeks, but only if she went ahead to America and established a home for you. That was when she wrote to tell me that she was leaving and would send for you as soon as she could."

"That was almost a year ago," I said, my eyes filling with tears.

. . . We were nearing the airport now, and the roadway was filled with vehicles of all sorts, pouring into the narrow lanes near the main building. On both sides of us there were hangars crowded with military planes, and on the runways ahead of us I could see several large American aircraft and people running toward them.

"Yes, that was in 1974, just about a year ago," Kim agreed. "I did not want to tell you anything until I knew for certain that you would be allowed to leave Saigon. And that news came one month ago. It has taken weeks to find room for you on a plane. They are all jammed with people trying to escape from the war. I've been told that the price of a ticket has risen so high that it costs a fortune to buy a seat on a plane. The United States government is paying for yours, and that is why you are able to leave."

Kim Be made her way through the crowds as I held onto the seat in front of me.

"Stay close to me once we leave the bicycle," she instructed. "We have some distance to go, I think, and I do not know my way very well."

Leaving the bicycle at a stall and carefully locking it in place, Kim Be motioned me to walk with her. I carried my sleeping mat and clutched my little cloth sack. Hurrying through the entrance doors, we entered a large building bursting with refugees, police, military guards, animals, packing crates, and sandbag barricades.

I looked around us, at the hundreds of Vietnamese children gathered in little clusters, while women and young girls watched over them.

"They are all waiting," Kim Be said. "Waiting for a plane to anywhere."

"You must think just one thing, dear one," Kim whispered. "You must think of how wonderful it will be to see your mother again. It has been so long. And remember, it has not been easy for her to have been separated from you for three years. She waits for you, San Ho."

Kim Be pulled me close to her and held me as she

kissed my cheek again and again. We said nothing for the longest while, and I could feel her breath on my face and then her tears. Finally, she released me.

"Go now, my brave one," Kim whispered, as a woman came toward me with an American comic book in her hand.

The woman's face was kind, and she smiled as she handed me the book. Then, after tying a tag onto my tunic, she guided me toward the gate where I had waited for the plane the week before. This time the plane would not have too many people, I told myself. This time I would not be turned away.

Walking toward the gate, I paused and looked back at the crowd of people standing near Kim Be. For a very long minute I stared at her, wanting so much to run to her—to hold onto her and feel her strength and reassuring words. I felt a slight tug on my arm, and the kind woman began to guide me through the gate once again and out into the hot April sun.

We walked across the runway toward the plane, big and shiny as it rested on the tarmac. A stairway led up to a doorway, and there were people standing at the entrance, all of them wearing uniforms.

The woman led me up the steps and into the plane, where many children—each with little white tags like mine—sat together, several in each seat. There were nurses standing in the aisles, and two doctors with name plates on their white suits bent over the smaller children, speaking softly to them as they adjusted blankets, stroked their arms, and placed small toys near each one.

I saw children of all ages as I walked down the aisle. There were babies holding bottles, and boys and girls who looked my age, twelve or so. Several young girls sat together, talking excitedly to each other.

My seat was near a window, and I shared it with a boy who was much younger than I. His face was swollen and he looked as though he had been crying for a long time. I asked him his name, and he tried to speak but couldn't. I put my arm out to him, and he moved toward me.

"I know how you feel," I said. "I'm afraid, too."

Several of the women walked down the aisle, stopping at each seat to buckle us into the seat belts. The plane began to move slowly down the runway and, as it turned onto a long strip of tarmac, the schoolgirls near me became silent. Suddenly, we started to gain tremendous speed and the engines roared.

My heart pounded in my ears as I grabbed the little boy next to me. Slowly the plane left the ground and began to climb into the air. Tan Son Nhut airfield sank beneath us, getting smaller and smaller as I watched from my window.

Turning my head toward the children all around me, I felt terribly alone. Three years had passed since I had last seen my mother. Three years had passed since I had stood in front of the house in Saigon and watched her move silently down the street and away from me.

What would it be like in America? Would my mother really be there to meet me? Would the American she had married be kind to me?

I leaned my head against the seat and closed my eyes. I felt very tired. It all seemed so far away. America. My mother. And a country across the sea, on the other side of the world.

. . . Our plane started to make a circle. We could see the airport now, and the landing field with its lines of red lights. Everyone stopped talking. I could hardly breathe. My stomach felt tight, and I reached out to the boy. We sat there, holding onto each other and staring at the red lights.

Suddenly, the plane was on the ground, and the engine roared as we raced down the runway and came to a stop. I could feel perspiration on my face.

I clung to the boy, who was shaking now and saying something that I could not understand.

A crowd gathered on the ground outside our plane. Lights were flashing on and off as people began to take pictures like they had done in San Francisco. I unfastened my seat belt and bent under me to find my little cloth sack and my rolled up sleeping mat. I reached for the small book that the woman at the Saigon airport had given me and tucked it into my sack.

I stood up as everyone started to move toward the front of the plane. A nurse stepped forward and motioned that I was to follow her along with others who had left the plane with me. Unaccustomed to the chill, I shuddered beneath my black tunic, pulling it closer around me as we moved along in exhausted, fearful silence. The small child next to me whimpered and rubbed at eyes that were swollen and reddened with tears.

Suddenly, I heard voices talking all at once, some of them shouting at us as the lights from a thousand cameras flashed all over the area through which we walked. Some of the children covered their faces with one hand as they clung to a toy or a book that had been given to them at the airport in Saigon. Others stared straight ahead as they shuffled along, strangers in a sea of strangers. One of the photographers cut in front of the children just ahead of me, thrusting his camera in front of my face and speaking the language I recognized from the soldiers in Saigon. I turned my head quickly to the left to avoid him, only to be confronted with a dozen more cameras, the lights from their flashes sending darts of pain through my eyes.

At last we came into an enormous room where crowds of people waited, talking and shouting in this language I could not understand. What were they saying? Where was I being taken? And what would happen if I lost sight of my group and the nurse who had brought us from the plane? I wondered how my mother would possibly find me in the midst of all of these strangers.

Then the nurse who was in charge of my group took us to a line of tables where men and women sat taking from us the papers that had been pushed into our hands as we went through the gates at the airport in Saigon. After a few minutes, we were taken to a second group of tables piled high with clothing. A lady smiled at me and said something that I could not understand. She handed me a small blue jacket from across the table. It looked warm and was much like the clothing I had seen in the windows in Saigon. I nodded my head to show my thanks and quickly wrapped the jacket around my shoulders to take away the chill of the air.

Then I was led through crowds of people calling out to each other and taking pictures of all of us. Everywhere I looked were the faces of strangers, and my head throbbed with the noise and the confusion. And then, at last, I heard my mother's voice.

"San Ho!" she cried out to me, laughing and crying as I saw her among the people. Leaving my group, I ran toward her, weaving in and out of the crowd until I reached her, throwing my arms around her neck as she grabbed me and held me close to her.

I held onto my mother for some time. I can still hear her speaking softly to me as she stroked my hair and pressed her wet cheek to mine. All about us, people were picking up the children who had come with me on the plane. I no longer heard the noise—only my mother's voice as it soothed my fright and my confusion.

Then I saw the American. He was standing apart from us. He was much bigger than my mother. He was broad-shouldered and wore the uniform of the Marines stationed in Saigon, not that of the Marines who searched the huts in our village. The American stepped forward now and came closer to my mother, extending a hand toward me. I looked up into his eyes, which were framed by heavy-rimmed glasses. I stood there, looking at the American and then into the face of my mother. Who is this stranger? I thought, who married my mother and took her so far away from my land, to this country on the other side of the world?

I looked once more at the American and tried to manage a smile, but the smile would not come. I tried to move toward the man but I couldn't. My whole body was frozen with fear.

BLUE SKYE

by
Lael Littke

I f it hadn't been for her knowledge that her mother, Reanna, and Bill were really going to try to leave her, Skye would have enjoyed the wedding. It began with a procession, led by two girls playing flutes. They wore flower garlands on their heads like Reanna's and Skye's. Next came Reanna and Bill, followed by Bill's friend who'd bought the motorcycles, then Skye and Grandpa who smelled of shaving lotion and Listerine. He walked stiffly, as if he disapproved of the whole thing, which Skye knew he did.

Then there were all the aunts, uncles, and those Cousins by the Dozens. Denise was there in a cream-colored dress that made her black hair look even darker, and Lee Esther was there, too, in a blue dress that didn't do a whole lot for her pale brown hair and sunburned skin. Both of them had their hair sprayed so much that it stood out around their faces like wire. Both of them wore nylons and white shoes with little heels.

Looking at them Skye felt like a geek in the droopy long dress and her floppy old sandals. But

Cody, the tall guy-cousin who'd been nice to her at Aunt Esta's, grinned and winked at her, which made her feel a little better. There was another guy with Cody, younger, about Skye's age, with red hair and freckles. He glanced at Skye and blushed.

She guessed that he must be one of the neighbor's kids.

The other wedding guests trailed behind the relatives. Jermer Golightly and Sweetie Farnsworth were back there somewhere. Jermer wore a tight-fitting dark blue suit with too-short sleeves. For once he didn't have his backpack with him. Sweetie was dressed in something magenta-colored and flowing, a lot different from the pale, flowered dresses the aunts wore. Her hair, which was a mixture of blonde and gray, was done up in a smooth lump at the back of her head. She seemed a lot younger than the aunts.

They all walked across Grandpa's wide lawn and down the long shady lane that led to the creek. The flutes played something light and happy that made you want to dance. Except that Skye felt too heavy to dance. Heavy with the knowledge that Bill didn't want her along. It began to hurt now, like when you pound a finger but there's no pain right at first. Then, just when you think, "Well, that wasn't so bad," it pounces on you and makes you scream.

Bill didn't want her, and Reanna was willing to toss her away like those pictures from the past that she'd got rid of.

Well, Skye didn't care. She'd show them all. They weren't going to get away with this. She had a secret of her own.

She clumped along, hitching up the neck of her dress and thinking angrily about how she was going to let off quite a mouthful when they got to that part of the marriage ceremony about speak now or forever hold your peace. She'd seen weddings on the TV soap operas she and Reanna watched. She'd wait until they asked if anybody knew a reason why this marriage shouldn't happen. Then she'd really let them have it.

She scarcely noticed when Sweetie Farnsworth caught up with her.

"That scooped neck is going to scoop right down to your belly button if you're not careful," Sweetie whispered. Skillfully she pulled the front of the dress together and fastened it with an old-fashioned brooch she'd been wearing on her own dress. "Now you look like a bridesmaid," she whispered as she dropped back to join Jermer.

The ceremony was short. It took place under a bower of willows by the creek. Several cows and a couple of horses watched from behind a fence across the creek. That skinny black and white cat was there, too, roosting on the trunk of a fallen tree where it had a good view of everything.

Back at the house Tarzan barked, unhappy about being left behind.

Reanna and Bill stood together under the willows,

with Bill's friend on one side and Skye on the other. They said some poetry to one another and exchanged wedding rings while Skye held Reanna's bouquet. Then they signed some papers that an official-looking man had brought. That's all there was to it. They were married. Nobody even said anything about speaking now or forever holding your peace.

Bewildered, Skye walked behind the newlyweds back to the lawn where the aunts and uncles and Cousins by the Dozens and other guests swarmed over the food tables, squawking like the magpies that picked through Grandpa's manure pile by the barn.

The cousin named Cody had some pieces of cardboard and a big felt pen.

"Let's make some 'Just Married' signs, Skye," he said, giving her the pen. "We can tie them to the motorcycles."

Skye had no interest in making signs, but she took the piece of cardboard Cody held out to her and started printing.

Denise and Lee Esther and several younger cousins watched.

It made Skye nervous. Her hand shook.

She'd just finished printing one sign when Denise poked Lee Esther and said in a loud whisper, "Maybe they don't teach spelling in Ten Sleep and Tombstone and those other fancy places she's been."

Lee Esther tossed her pale, stiff hair and smiled. "Denise's the spelling champion of the whole county," she said, as if that meant something great.

Skye looked at the sign and saw she'd printed, "Just Marred." How could she have done anything that dumb right in front of the cousins?

"You can fix that easy," Cody said.

But Skye handed him the pen. "You fix it." She couldn't keep her mind on dumb signs. Reanna and Bill would be leaving soon.

She hurried upstairs where she took off the green dress and the garland and put on her jeans and old red plaid shirt. That was what she always wore for traveling. She put the garland of flowers back on her head. That would remind Reanna of all the years they'd traveled together, stopping to pick roadside flowers and braid them together.

Shoving her few possessions into her duffel, Skye started downstairs. She wasn't even halfway down when she heard the engines of the black-and-silver Harleys rev up.

"Skye," she heard Reanna call. "Skye, come say good-bye."

Skye clattered down the rest of the stairs. "I'm coming, Reanna," she yelled. "Wait for me."

The cycles were already moving by the time she got out to the yard.

"Wait," she screamed. "I'm going with you."

"Come give me a hug," Reanna said, reaching out her arms. Skye plunged into them. "Hey, pal," Reanna whispered in her ear, "I sure love ya."

"How much?" This was another of their old games.

It was a baby game, but Skye wanted to jog Reanna's memory about all those things they'd shared.

Reanna laughed softly.

"As much as from here to Tincup, Colorado. This is hard, honeybun. We've never been apart before." Reanna tried to pry Skye off her. Reanna never was much of a toucher.

But Skye clung to her, still clutching her duffel. "Take me with you. I can't stay here."

"Yes, you can. Now smile, Skye, and tell me you're happy for me." Reanna unwound her arms. For just a moment she looked into her eyes and Skye thought she was going to relent and say, "Aw, what the heck. Hop on behind me."

But all she said was, "Good-bye, Skye. Good-bye, my dearie, my daughter."

Now Skye was supposed to say, "Good-bye, my mother, my dear."

But she wasn't going to say that now. That was for when Reanna went to work and would be home at the end of the day.

"Good-bye, Skye," Bill echoed.

The motorcycles started rolling again.

Dumping the duffel, Skye ran after them wailing, "I'm not staying. I'm not staying." She even got a leg up on Reanna's cycle, but Bill reached over and gently lifted her off.

"Sorry, Blue Skye," he said with that big goofy grin she used to like. "No kids allowed on the honeymoon." Reaching behind him, he pulled a new map of the western states from a pocket on his cycle. "Here, you can follow us on this map. We'll let you know where we're heading."

He thrust it into Skye's hand and hugged her.

She yanked away. She didn't want his hugs and she didn't want his stupid map. She picked it up and threw it back at him. "I've already got a map," she yelled.

"Skye, listen," Reanna said without stopping her motorcycle. "Get acquainted with the cousins and everybody, and you'll hardly notice we're gone. We'll be back soon."

"How soon?" Skye demanded. "Soon" was an elastic word with Reanna that could stretch to mean any amount of time she wanted it to mean. "Three days? Four?"

"Soon," Reanna repeated. "We'll be in touch. Be happy, Skye."

Then they were gone in a thunder of vrooms and clouds of dust. . . .

Skye planned to cry all night long.

She tried hard as she lay in her bed in the narrow, slant-ceilinged upstairs room, but after a few dry sobs she gave it up. She wasn't a crier. Just because she'd cried when Reanna and Bill rode away didn't mean she was a wimpy weeper. She'd had a good reason to cry. Even old spelling champ Denise would have cried if her mother had left her behind.

She stared into the darkness, hanging onto the thought that Reanna and Bill would be back in three or four days. But she was the one who said they'd be back then. Not Reanna. She didn't think Reanna would have made it such a big secret if they were going to be gone only three or four days.

What if they were gone a month?

Skye groaned.

What she really should do was figure out how to catch up to them. They wouldn't be going far that night, especially since it was starting to rain.

She and Reanna had passed a pretty place to camp alongside Bear River on the day they'd arrived in Sheep Creek. It was just a few miles away on the road to Preston. That's probably where Reanna and

Bill would be camping, at least that night.

If she could find them and showed up right at their tent, they wouldn't turn her away. Or would they?

An imagined scene of them pushing her out of their tent into the darkness almost brought the tears. She thought of the "Fanged Haunts" Reanna used to tell her about when she was small. They were creatures that inhabited the darkness beyond the campfire, ready to gobble up foolish children who wandered away from safety. She wasn't quite sure what Fanged Haunts were supposed to look like, but Reanna had said they were out there, with gaping, fanged mouths ready.

She imagined Reanna and Bill throwing her out of the tent, with the Fanged Haunts there, waiting, their eyes glowing like stars and their breath whispering in and out like the night wind in the trees.

One big sob was all she could manage. She tried to stay awake and figure out how she could go after Reanna. Forget Bill. She'd just ignore him.

But the bed was firm and comfortable, not at all like the squashy, lumpy cots in the rented rooms where she and Reanna had lived. The sheets were crisp and smelled of sunshine and fresh air, not stale like the old sleeping bags they'd used when they camped.

She slept.

She woke in the morning to the sound of raindrops on the roof. She lay there looking at the daisies on the pale green wallpaper and thinking of

Reanna and Bill camped somewhere in the rain, soggy and miserable. But then she remembered the cozy days she and Reanna had spent in their tent, playing games, talking, making plans while the rain pattered against the canvas.

Suddenly she felt as dismal as the day.

Then she heard the sound that told her how she could escape to go looking for Reanna and Bill. Grandpa was bringing the full milk cans to the roadside where Mr. Jensen, the milk hauler, would pick them up. Sometimes people used Mr. Jensen's truck like a bus service, riding into Preston with him to do some shopping, then riding home with him on his return trip.

Skye had met Mr. Jensen twice in the week she'd been in Sheep Creek. He would let her ride along with him, and she'd see those black-and-silver Harleys somewhere along the way.

She'd better not tell Grandpa. He'd probably be happy to have her leave, but he'd feel it was his duty to stop her. She and Reanna could call him later from town.

Now that she had a plan, Skye jumped out of bed, and looked right into the face of a Fanged Haunt that perched on the windowsill, on the other side of the glass. That's what it had to be, sitting there dripping and ugly in the rain with its open mouth displaying small but nasty fangs.

"Reanna, help!" Skye whispered through a dry throat.

The Fanged Haunt disappeared, but not before Skye saw it was just the skinny black and white cat again, the one that had been watching her since she came.

She ran to the window, feeling embarrassed, as if somebody had caught her believing in the tooth fairy. The cat stood on a limb of the huge tree just outside the window, and again it opened its mouth in a silent meow.

"Here, kitty, kitty." Skye pushed up the window, but the cat skittered down the trunk of the tree and vanished in the rain.

Mr. Jensen's milk truck went by on its way to the farms on the north end of the village, which meant Skye had about an hour to get ready to leave. That was plenty of time.

She got dressed, once again putting on her traveling outfit of jeans, red plaid shirt, and sneakers. Her duffel was still packed from yesterday. On her way downstairs, she stashed it along with her map of the western states and her denim jacket on the landing.

Grandpa was just sitting down at the kitchen table with his newspaper. "Well, good morning, Sis," he said when he saw her.

This was the first time the two of them had had breakfast alone. He looked as if he was trying to think of something else to say. Finally he said, "Better have some breakfast," and unfolded the newspaper, which he put up in front of his face.

"I will." She didn't mind that he hid behind the

newspaper. That way he wouldn't notice if she looked flushed or excited. She hoped he'd go back to the barn before Mr. Jensen returned. "Aren't you going to eat, Grandpa?" she asked.

"Yes, I am, Sis." Grandpa's arm snaked out from behind the newspaper. He picked up a bowl from the stack that always sat on the table, then fumbled for one of the cereal boxes that were also stored there.

Breakfast with Grandpa was simply taking your pick of the many boxes of cereal that occupied half of the light-colored oval table. Twice since Skye and Reanna had been there Aunt Esta had come over and put all of the cereal boxes inside one of the cupboards. Both times, as soon as she'd gone, Grandpa took them all out again and put them back on the table.

Skye took a bowl from the stack and looked over the selection of cereal. There were Shredded Wheat and Corn Flakes and All-Bran and some others equally dull. Grandpa didn't go for the interesting ones like Cocoa Puffs and Cinnamon Toast Crunch, although Skye'd found a box of Crispy Critters.

After a look out the window to make sure Mr. Jensen wasn't coming back yet, she filled her bowl half full of Crispy Critters and added milk from the thick white pitcher that stood on the table. Milk from Grandpa's own cows. She poured some on Grandpa's All-Bran, too.

"Jittery, Sis?" Grandpa asked suddenly, and Skye was aware that she'd been drumming her fingers while she ate her cereal.

She'd better act casual while she listened for Mr. Jensen's truck.

Clearing her throat, she said, "Grandpa, do you know where that cat lives? That scrawny one that hangs around and watches us?"

Grandpa was hiding behind his newspaper again. "Probably nowhere," he said around it.

"But it must live somewhere. Where did it come from if nobody owns it?"

"Sometimes people drop their unwanted animals off along the road. Danged fools think somebody will take them in, but there are too many of them." Grandpa lowered the newspaper a little. "Cat's just a stray. Lucky one at that, if Tarzan hasn't torn it apart."

Skye was horrified. "Would he do that?"

"Dunno. Doesn't generally take to having strays on his turf." Grandpa went back to reading his paper.

Did Grandpa resent having strays on his turf, too?

Well, she wouldn't be there much longer. Skye shoved the rest of her cereal into her mouth. It was stale, like the others in the boxes on the table. How long had they been sitting there? How long did it take for one person to eat through nine boxes of cereal all by himself?

Maybe she'd ought to offer to fix breakfast for

Grandpa. She and Reanna had invented some great things, like Cheese Monster, which was a Bisquick biscuit topped with Velveeta cheese and a fried egg. She knew how to make that.

But it wouldn't be fair to get Grandpa used to good cooking when she was cutting out. Besides, there wasn't time now.

Grandpa put down his newspaper and pushed his chair back, the legs scraping against the linoleum floor. "Got work to do out in the barn." Standing, he looked at Skye as if he were trying again to think of more to say. "See you later, Sis," he said, and left.

"Good-bye, Grandpa." Skye hoped he'd stay inside the barn so he wouldn't see her getting into

the milk truck. She'd leave him a note. He'd understand how it was.

As she swallowed her last Crispy Critter, Skye saw the black and white cat loft itself to the windowsill outside. She was glad to know Tarzan hadn't gotten it.

The cat carried something in her mouth, something small and wet and bedraggled. A kitten! The skinny cat had a kitten.

"Oh, babe!" Skye murmured, leaping to her feet and hurrying outside. What if Tarzan should come before she got to the cat? Could he put his big paws up on the sill and snatch both the mother and the kitten?

Tarzan was nowhere in sight, but that didn't mean he couldn't show up at any moment.

The cat allowed Skye to pick her up and carry her inside, still holding the dripping kitten by the scruff of its neck. Skye put the cat down on the kitchen floor. Only then did the cat let go of the kitten, setting it down gently on its sturdy little legs.

The kitten was small. Skye didn't know a whole lot about cats, but she thought it was probably close to a month old. The marks on its face gave it a funny, surprised look. The black and white on its back made it look as if it were wearing overalls.

It stood there bewildered, turning its head and mewing in high-pitched squeaks.

Skye thought it was the most beautiful thing she'd ever seen. She'd never had a pet. "Pets are a nuisance," Reanna had said. "They tie you down."

There'd been that time they'd rented a room in a big two-story house in Wyoming, a house that had been full of kids and animals. The family cat had kittens, three bright orange and white ones, and one little tiger-striped gray one with green eyes. Skye had loved that little gray cat and had begged Reanna to let her take him when they left. Reanna explained patiently that the way they lived, traveling from place to place in the old station wagon, was no life for a kitten, that it needed cat food they couldn't afford, that taking on a responsibility like that was limiting their freedom.

Skye had said a tearful good-bye to the gray kitten when Reanna got bored with the waitress job she'd taken at a cafe in town and said it was time to move on. The kids at the house said they didn't know anybody who wanted a kitten. Their faces had been gloomy when they said it, as if they knew what happened to unwanted kittens. Skye hadn't wanted to know.

The skinny cat was licking her baby, glancing up now and then at Skye. She made soft, proud sounds, which Skye interpreted as meaning, "Isn't it splendid? Isn't it the most beautiful kitten you ever saw?"

Skye plopped down on the floor and reached out to pet the mother cat's wet fur. She was shocked at how thin the cat was. "Hey babe," she said. "You're just skin and bones." That was what Aunt Esta had said about her. "I'll get you something to eat."

But the cat wanted out. Walking over to the door, she meowed politely.

Skye got up. "You're going to run off without your baby? You're like somebody else I could name."

The cat threaded herself through Skye's feet, rubbing washboard ribs against her legs.

"Okay, if that's what you want." Skye opened the door and the cat dashed off in the rain.

It was then that she heard Mr. Jensen's truck coming back down the road.

"Hey, come back," she yelled at the cat. "I can't baby-sit for you. I have to go."

But the cat was gone.

Skye turned to look at the kitten who took trembling steps toward nowhere. It mewed frantically. Skye picked it up, making soft, soothing sounds.

The kitten was a male. The kids in that two-story house in Wyoming had taught her how to tell. He fit perfectly into her palm. She stroked his back with a gentle finger.

"I'll just have to put you back outside, I guess," she said.

But Tarzan might get him.

The kitten smelled clean, like the hay in Grandpa's barn. That must have been where the mother cat had been keeping him. Maybe she should take him back there.

But the barn wasn't safe with Tarzan there, which was probably why the mother cat had brought him to the house.

The milk truck was at the neighbor's place now. Skye could hear the whine of the lift that hoisted the heavy cans to the bed of the truck.

If she didn't go with Mr. Jensen this morning, Reanna and Bill would probably move on. To where? Which direction would they be going? How could she find them?

She peered through the rain, looking for the mother cat. "Kitty, kitty," she called.

The cat was nowhere in sight. Skye would just have to leave the kitten there in the kitchen and hope for the best.

Putting him back on the floor, she hurried to the stair landing for her things. She pulled on her denim jacket, grabbed her map, and threw the duffel over her shoulder. As she went out, she left the door open so the mother cat could get back in to her kitten.

Mr. Jensen's truck stopped at the end of the driveway to pick up Grandpa's milk cans.

Behind Skye the kitten mewed. She looked back. He stood alone on the doorsill, turning his head, blurry blue eyes searching. Was he trying to follow her?

She couldn't just leave him there. But he was too small to take with her.

Well, so the world was a hard place.

Mr. Jensen slammed a door as he got out of the truck. The noise must have frightened the kitten because he skittered back into the kitchen, still mewing.

Skye began to run toward the milk truck. "Mr. Jensen," she called.

Tarzan came from the barn to deliver a friendly bark at Mr. Jensen then looked curiously toward the house. Could he hear the kitten's tiny cries?

Skye stopped. She'd have to shut the kitchen door so Tarzan couldn't get in.

But then the mother cat couldn't get in either. Would Tarzan grab the cat while she tried to get to her baby?

Mr. Jensen looked toward Skye. "Did you want something, Skye?"

Maybe Reanna and Bill would stay put for a day or two since it was raining so hard. Maybe she could catch up with them tomorrow.

"Just wanted to say hello," Skye yelled to Mr. Jensen, then turned back toward the house.

Behind her, Skye heard Mr. Jensen's truck start up. She thought of it going down the road, past the dripping willows that lined the creek bank, past the church and the school and the general store, past the gray cliffs that jutted out toward the river. That's where she was sure Bill and Reanna would be camped, there under the giant box elder trees by the riverside, where they could hear the whisper of the water as they ate breakfast in their tent. Maybe they had cooked bacon in the shelter of the big trees over Reanna's little one-burner propane stove. The smell of it would be strong in the tent, along with the odors of the canvas and the freshness of the rain-filled air.

So what was Skye doing here, worrying about a dumb kitten? Why hadn't she believed Reanna, who'd said so many times that pets tie you down, limit your freedom, get in your way?

Skye was almost back to the kitchen door when Jermer Golightly suddenly appeared. He slogged through the rain juggling a huge black umbrella, his blue backpack, and an armful of boxes.

Great. That's just what she needed. Somebody who sang mournful songs and liked funerals.

Maybe he'd like to hold a funeral for her hopes.

Tarzan came over to wag his tail as a greeting to Jermer, then went back to the barn.

"Hi," Jermer said to Skye. "Want to play Boggle? I don't know how to spell many words, but I like to play."

Now Skye saw that the boxes Jermer carried were games. Monopoly. Clue. Scrabble. Some others whose titles she couldn't see.

"No," she said.

"How about Rook? Or Go Fish? I've got Pit, too, and Uno." Jermer followed her inside the kitchen, taking a while to get the big umbrella through the door, then kicking the door shut behind him. He stopped short when he heard the kitten mewing. Spotting him there in the middle of the floor, Jermer dropped the umbrella and tossed his backpack and armload of games on the table, falling to his knees beside the kitten. "Skye, where did you get him?"

"His mother dumped him on me," Skye said.

Jermer reached out a hand to stroke the mewing kitten. "He's so scared. Is it all right if I pick him up?"

Skye shrugged. "I couldn't care less."

Why was she angry at the kitten? He couldn't help being dumped any more than she could.

"He'd probably like it," she said in a kinder voice.

Jermer picked the kitten up, cradling him against his chest. "Oh, oh, oh," he crooned. "Oh, oh, oh." He looked at Skye. "What's his name?"

"You just named him," Skye said. "We'll call him Oh."

"Oh," Jermer sang. "Oh, Oh, Oh." It was the tune from the funeral song Jermer liked to sing.

"Want him?" Skye asked.

For a moment Jermer's face lit up, but then he said, "I couldn't take him to Sweetie's house. Old Mangler would chew him up."

Mangler was Sweetie Farnsworth's old tomcat. Skye had seen him, a battered orange warrior with half a tail and one droopy ear. Sweetie said she'd found him somewhere, hurt, near death, and had brought him home to see what she could do. Now he was fat and lazy and jealous of his territory.

Like Tarzan.

What difference did it make whether Mangler chewed up the kitten or if Tarzan got to him first?

"Besides," Jermer said, "He's too young to be away from his mother."

"His mother's gone," Skye said.

Jermer held the kitten against his cheek and smiled, a soft, sweet smile. "She'll come back," he said. "Cats always do."

As if in answer to his certainty, there was a meow at the door. Skye hurried over to open it. The scrawny cat picked up a kitten she'd apparently dropped so she could meow, and brought it inside. Setting it down at Skye's feet, she looked up.

"Sure," Skye said. "Why not? You've already ruined my life. I might as well take in another kitten."

Despite her harsh words, she knelt to look at the new arrival. This one was smaller than Oh, but it stood its ground silently, and when Skye touched it gently, it opened its tiny mouth and hissed.

Skye fell instantly, hopelessly in love. "Oh, you little thing," she said. "You sassy little thing."

She picked up the kitten. Like the other one, this one was mostly black, but it had a white face and chest and a little black chin which gave it a flower look. It stood on Skye's palm and stared at her through blue eyes blurred with babyhood. It hissed again.

"No bigger than a Twinkie, but ready to fight," Skye said.

That's what she'd name this one. Twinkie. When Reanna saw the spirit of the little thing, she'd let her keep it. Reanna admired spirit, especially in females. Skye checked and wasn't surprised to find that's what this kitten was. Surely Reanna would say they had to keep this one.

This book was set in Caslon 224 Book
and composed by Robin D'Amato.
It was printed on 50 lb. Finch Opaque.
Cover illustration by Donna Perrone.
Title page illustration by Chi Chung.

———

Editor: Deborah Jerome-Cohen
Design: Patricia Isaza
Cover Design: Patricia Isaza